Readers
LEVEL 2

Looking After Me

Keeping
Healthy

Sally Hewitt

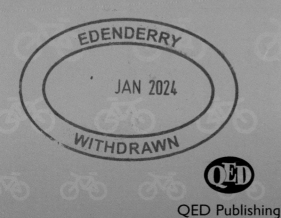

QED Publishing

First published in the UK in 2014 by
QED Publishing
A Quarto Group company
The Old Brewery
6 Blundell Street
London N7 9BH

www.qed-publishing.co.uk

Designed by Astwood Design

A catalogue record for this book is available from the British Library.

ISBN 978 1 78171 549 9

Printed in China

Picture credits

(t = top, b = bottom, l = left, r = right, fc = front cover)

Shutterstock fc Monkey Business Images, 4 2xSamara.com, 5tl Samuel Borges
Photography, 5br Anton Havelaar, 6b Ljupco Smokovski, 6-7 Monkey Business Images,
8-9 Anelina, 9tl Robyn Mackenzie, 9tr Yasonya, 9br donfiore, 10 Nanette Grebe, 10-11
jordache, 12-13 Gladskikh Tatiana, 14-15 greenland, 16-17 Sergey Novikov, 16l Coprid,
16cl auremar, 16cr gorillaimages, 16r George Dolgikh, 17 stockyimages, 18 Lusoimages,
19b s_oleg, 20 Bronwyn Photo, 21 wavebreakmedia, 22 lukaszfus, 23l Thomas M Perkins

Words in **bold** can be found in the Glossary on page 24.

Contents

Your body

Your body is amazing. It can think and learn, run and play.

It can see, hear, smell, taste and feel.

5

To help your
body to grow and
stay **healthy**,
you need to look
after yourself.

Eat well

Food gives your body **energy**.

You need energy for everything that you do.

If you don't eat and drink enough, you will soon feel tired.

You need to eat fresh food and plenty of fruit and vegetables. These are very good for you. "Yum, Yum"

Drink lots of water during the day.

Keep moving

Moving helps keep your **muscles** and bones strong.

It makes your **heart** and **lungs** work harder.

10

Your blood flows more quickly and you breathe in more air.

Moving is fun! You can walk, run, climb and swim. You can play sports and games.

Fight germs

Germs are too small to see, but they can make you ill.

If you are ill, stay warm and rest. This helps your body to fight germs and get better.

13

Germs can get on your hands.

Make sure that you wash your hands before you eat.

Enjoy fresh air

Sunshine and fresh air
help to keep you healthy.

But hot sun can burn your skin,
so wear sunscreen and a hat.

When it is cold outside, wrap up warmly before you go out.

Getting too cold makes you shiver!

Stay clean

During the day, your body gets dirty.

A bath or shower washes away dirt and germs and keeps you feeling fresh!

Brush your teeth every morning and evening to get rid of germs and bits of old food.

Sleep well

Your body works hard all day.

It works by thinking, moving eating and growing.

After that, it needs a long rest while you sleep.

You need to get plenty
of sleep to stay healthy.

When you get
up, you are
ready for
a new day.

Glossary

energy   the power needed by your body to move and grow

healthy   you are healthy when you are strong and well

heart   your heart pumps blood all around your body

lungs   you use your lungs to breathe. They suck air into your body and blow out used air.

muscles   the fleshy parts of your body that move the bones